MANGA SHAKE

KING LEAR

ADAPTED BY
RICHARD APPIGNANESI

ILLUSTRATED BY
ILYA

SELF
MADE
HERO

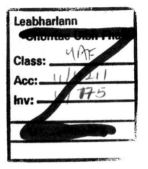

SELF MADE HERO

Published by
SelfMadeHero
A division of Metro Media Ltd
5 Upper Wimpole Street
London W1G 6BP
www.selfmadehero.com

This edition published 2009

Illustrator: Ilya
Text Adaptor: Richard Appignanesi
Designer: Andy Huckle
Textual Consultant: Nick de Somogyi
Publishing Director: Emma Hayley
With thanks to: Doug Wallace

ISBN: 978-0-9558169-7-0

10 9 8 7 6 5 4 3 2 1
Printed and bound in China

1759: The American wilderness near the shores of the Horican, or "Holy Lake", prosaically called "Lake George" by the English...

...Lear's kingdom.

The Fool

"Thou hast pared thy wit on both sides and left nothing in the middle!"

King Lear

"O let me not
be mad, not mad,
sweet heaven!"

Cordelia, Lear's youngest daughter

"O dear father, it is thy business that I go about!"

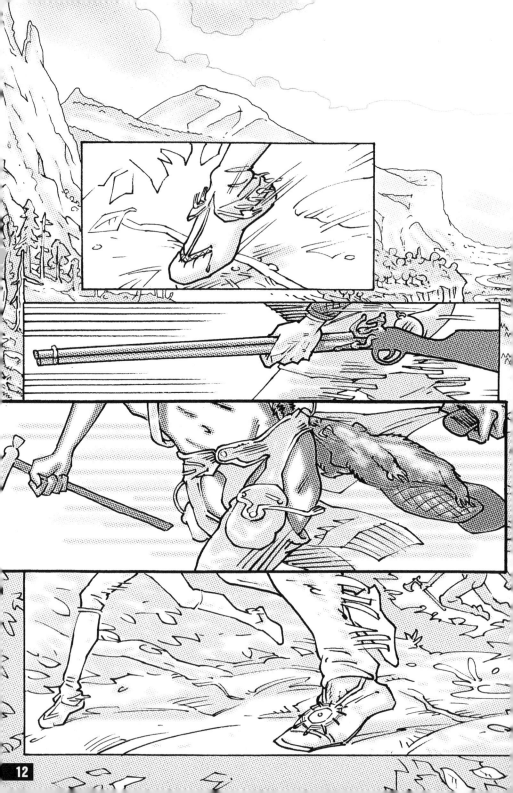

21

HERE'S FRANCE
AND BURGUNDY,
MY NOBLE
LORD.

53

...TO THAT ISSUE FOR WHICH I RAZED MY LIKENESS.

NOW, BANISHED KENT...

IF I OTHER ACCENTS BORROW, MY GOOD INTENT MAY CARRY THROUGH...

...IF THOU CANST SERVE, SO MAY THY MASTER FIND THEE FULL OF LABOURS.

LET ME NOT STAY A JOT FOR DINNER — GO GET IT READY...

...HOW NOW!

WHAT ART THOU?

A VERY HONEST-HEARTED FELLOW, AND AS POOR AS THE KING.

IF THOU BE AS POOR FOR A SUBJECT AS HE'S FOR A KING, THOU ART POOR ENOUGH.

...BUT YOU HAVE THAT IN YOUR COUNTENANCE WHICH I WOULD FAIN CALL MASTER.

WHAT'S THAT?

AUTHORITY.

DOST THOU KNOW ME, FELLOW?

NO, SIR...

63

NO, FAITH...

THEY'LL BE SNATCHING.

...LORDS AND GREAT MEN WILL NOT LET ME HAVE ALL THE FOOL TO MYSELF —

THOU HADST LITTLE WIT IN THY BALD CROWN...

...WHEN THOU GAV'ST THY GOLDEN ONE AWAY.

SIRRAH, WE'LL HAVE YOU WHIPPED.

THOU HAST PARED THY WIT ON BOTH SIDES...

...AND LEFT NOTHING IN THE MIDDLE.

80

85

87

97

'TIS WORSE THAN MURDER TO DO UPON RESPECT SUCH VIOLENT OUTRAGE.

NO.

YES.

WHERE IS THIS DAUGHTER?

HOW CHANCE THE KING COMES WITH SO SMALL A NUMBER?

IF THOU HADST BEEN SET IN THE STOCKS FOR THAT QUESTION, THOU'DST WELL DESERVED IT.

WHY, FOOL?

LET GO THY HOLD WHEN A GREAT WHEEL RUNS DOWN A HILL...

...LEST IT BREAK THY NECK WITH FOLLOWING IT.

O REGAN...

...WILT THOU TAKE HER BY THE HAND?

WHY NOT, SIR?

HOW HAVE I OFFENDED?

I PRAY YOU, FATHER...

...BEING WEAK...

...SEEM SO.

RETURN AND SOJOURN WITH MY SISTER.

RETURN TO HER, AND FIFTY MEN DISMISSED?

NO...

...RATHER I ABJURE ALL ROOFS, AND CHOOSE TO BE A COMRADE WITH THE WOLF AND OWL.

AT YOUR CHOICE, SIR.

IF YOU WILL COME TO ME, BRING BUT FIVE-AND-TWENTY.

FIFTY FOLLOWERS?

IS IT NOT WELL?

YEA...

...OR SO MANY?

I PRITHEE, DAUGHTER, DO NOT MAKE ME MAD.

WHAT SHOULD YOU NEED OF MORE?

TO NO MORE WILL I GIVE PLACE.

WHY MIGHT NOT YOU RECEIVE ATTENDANCE FROM THOSE THAT SHE CALLS SERVANTS, OR FROM MINE?

113

ALACK, EDMUND...

...I LIKE NOT THIS UNNATURAL DEALING!

WHEN I DESIRED THEIR LEAVE THAT I MIGHT PITY HIM...

...THEY CHARGED ME NEITHER TO SPEAK OF HIM NOR ANY WAY SUSTAIN HIM.

MOST SAVAGE AND UNNATURAL!

SAY YOU NOTHING.

THESE INJURIES THE KING NOW BEARS WILL BE REVENGED.

117

123

125

143

NOW, WHERE'S YOUR MASTER?

MADAM, WITHIN...

...BUT NEVER MAN SO CHANGED.

I TOLD HIM OF THE ARMY THAT WAS LANDED —

HE SMILED AT IT.

I TOLD HIM YOU WERE COMING —

HIS ANSWER WAS, "THE WORSE."

151

161

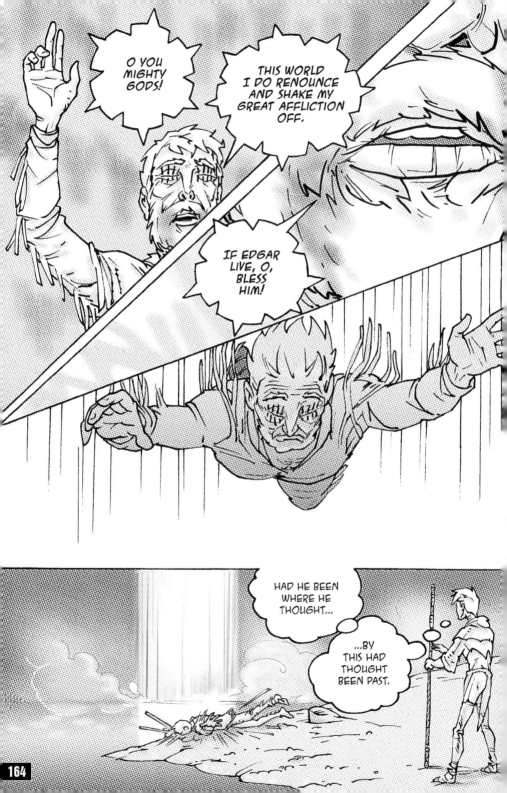

SLAVE...

...THOU HAST SLAIN ME.

GIVE THE LETTERS...

...TO EDMUND, EARL OF GLOUCESTER.

O, UNTIMELY DEATH!

I KNOW THEE WELL.

A SERVICEABLE VILLAIN, AS DUTEOUS TO THE VICES OF THY MISTRESS AS BADNESS WOULD DESIRE.

THESE LETTERS THAT HE SPEAKS OF MAY BE MY FRIENDS.

"Let our reciprocal vows be remembered. You have many opportunities to cut him off. There is nothing done if he return the conqueror. Then am I the prisoner, and his bed my jail, whereof deliver me, and supply the place for your labour.
Your (wife, so I would say) Affectionate Servant—
GONERIL"

A PLOT UPON HER VIRTUOUS HUSBAND'S LIFE...

...AND THE EXCHANGE MY BROTHER!

GIVE ME YOUR HAND.

FAR OFF I HEAR THE BEATEN DRUM.

181

I HEAR THE KING IS COME TO HIS DAUGHTER...

...WITH OTHERS WHOM THE RIGOUR OF OUR STATE FORCED TO CRY OUT.

IT TOUCHETH US AS FRANCE INVADES OUR LAND.

COMBINE TOGETHER AGAINST THE ENEMY...

...FOR THESE DOMESTIC BROILS ARE NOT THE QUESTION HERE.

LET'S THEN DETERMINE ON OUR PROCEEDING.

IF EVER YOUR GRACE HAD SPEECH WITH MAN SO POOR, HEAR ME ONE WORD.

SPEAK.

BEFORE YOU FIGHT THE BATTLE, OPE THIS LETTER.

WRETCHED THOUGH I SEEM...

...I CAN PRODUCE A CHAMPION THAT WILL PROVE WHAT IS AVOUCHED THERE.

STAY TILL I HAVE READ THE LETTER.

WHEN TIME SHALL SERVE...

...LET THE HERALD CRY, AND I'LL APPEAR AGAIN.

AWAY,
OLD MAN!

KING LEAR
HATH LOST...

"...HE AND HIS DAUGHTER TAKEN."

189

192

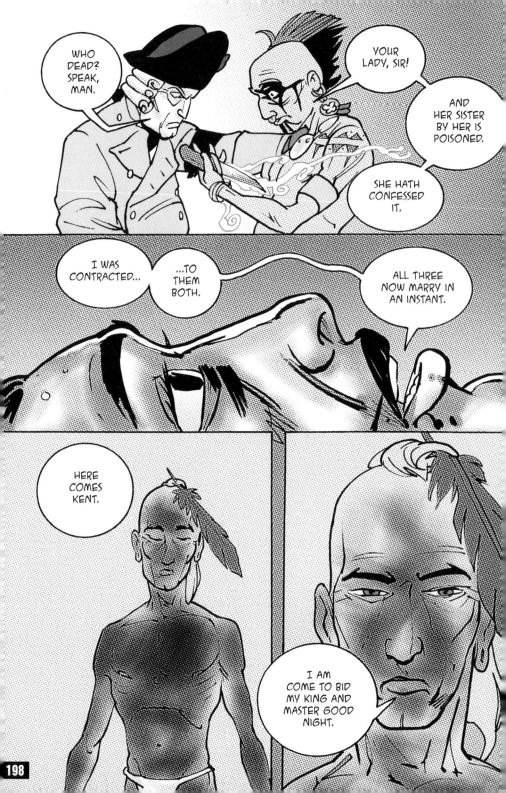

MY LORD, MY LORD!

VEX NOT HIS GHOST.

O, LET HIM PASS!

HE HATES HIM THAT WOULD UPON THE RACK OF THIS TOUGH WORLD STRETCH HIM OUT LONGER.

BEAR THEM FROM HENCE.

OUR PRESENT BUSINESS IS GENERAL WOE.

HE IS GONE INDEED.

THE WONDER IS, HE HATH ENDURED SO LONG.

FRIENDS OF MY SOUL...

...YOU TWAIN RULE IN THIS REALM.

203

PLOT SUMMARY OF KING LEAR

Old King Lear has three daughters: Goneril (wife of Albany), Regan (wife of Cornwall), and Cordelia (who has two suitors, Burgundy and France). Gloucester – Lear's counsellor, like him a widower – has two sons: Edgar, and the illegitimate Edmund. Lear has decided to abdicate, and divide his kingdom between his daughters, promising the largest portion to the one who loves him most. Goneril and Regan effusively declare their love, but Cordelia is revolted by this "love-test", replying that she loves him as any daughter should love a father. This enrages Lear, who disinherits her. Kent attempts to intervene – but is banished from the court. Burgundy withdraws his marriage offer, but Cordelia accepts that of France, and they leave together.

Now powerless, Lear is at the mercy of his elder daughters. When Goneril criticizes his behaviour, Lear angrily leaves to join Regan – but he is rapidly running out of friends. Only the Fool (his enigmatic court-jester) and the ever-faithful Kent (who has disguised himself to aid his master) stay loyal. When Kent arrives at Gloucester's castle, where Regan and Cornwall are staying, he is set in the stocks for insulting Goneril's servant Oswald. Lear is enraged at this – but then driven to madness when his two daughters unite against him. A storm breaks and he rages into the night, with only the Fool and Kent for company.

Meanwhile, Edmund has effected his plan to steal Edgar's inheritance by turning Gloucester against him. Edgar has fled, disguising himself as the madman "Poor Tom", and is seeking shelter in a countryside hovel during the storm when Lear, the Fool, and Kent arrive. Appalled at Regan and Goneril's behaviour, Gloucester seeks them out to offer the shelter of his castle. But Edmund betrays his father, and when Gloucester returns home, he is savagely punished by having his eyes put out. Kicked out of his own house, he is placed in the charge of the madman "Poor Tom" (his own disguised son Edgar). Assuming further rôles for his blind father, Edgar counsels him against despair.

Gloucester's blinding proves the turning-point: Cornwall is killed by an outraged servant (leaving Regan free to court Edmund); Albany vows revenge against Goneril (who has her eyes on Edmund herself); and Edgar kills Oswald when he tries to capture Gloucester. Cordelia lands with the French army, and is reunited with Lear, whom her doctor restores to sanity. But the French lose the battle, Cordelia and Lear are captured, and the terrible final phase begins.

Jealous of her relationship with Edmund, Goneril poisons Regan. In single combat, Edgar fatally wounds Edmund, to whom he reveals his identity, relating Gloucester's death from the shock at learning who "Poor Tom" really was. Goneril commits suicide. The dying Edmund reveals that he has ordered Lear and Cordelia's execution – but it is too late: Lear now enters with Cordelia's corpse, mad again with grief, and dies raving. Kent renounces the world; Lear's kingdom passes to Albany and Edgar.

A BRIEF LIFE OF WILLIAM SHAKESPEARE

Shakespeare's birthday is traditionally said to be the 23rd of April – St George's Day, patron saint of England. A good start for England's greatest writer. But that date and even his name are uncertain. He signed his own name in different ways. "Shakespeare" is now the accepted one out of dozens of different versions.

He was born at Stratford-upon-Avon in 1564, and baptized on 26th April. His mother, Mary Arden, was the daughter of a prosperous farmer. His father, John Shakespeare, a glove-maker, was a respected civic figure – and probably also a Catholic. In 1570, just as Will began school, his father was accused of illegal dealings. The family fell into debt and disrepute.

Will attended a local school for eight years. He did not go to university. The next ten years are a blank filled by suppositions. Was he briefly a Latin teacher, a soldier, a sea-faring explorer? Was he prosecuted and whipped for poaching deer?

We do know that in 1582 he married Anne Hathaway, eight years his senior, and three months pregnant. Two more children – twins – were born three years later but, by around 1590, Will had left Stratford to pursue a theatre career in London. Shakespeare's apprenticeship began as an actor and "pen for hire".

He learned his craft the hard way. He soon won fame as a playwright with often-staged popular hits.

He and his colleagues formed a stage company, the Lord Chamberlain's Men, which built the famous Globe Theatre. It opened in 1599 but was destroyed by fire in 1613 during a performance of *Henry VIII* which used gunpowder special effects. It was rebuilt in brick the following year.

Shakespeare was a financially successful writer who invested his money wisely in property. In 1597, he bought an enormous house in Stratford, and in 1608 became a shareholder in London's Blackfriars Theatre. He also redeemed the family's honour by acquiring a personal coat of arms.

Shakespeare wrote over 40 works, including poems, "lost" plays and collaborations, in a career spanning nearly 25 years. He retired to Stratford in 1613, where he died on 23rd April 1616, aged 52, apparently of a fever after a "merry meeting" of drinks with friends. Shakespeare did in fact die on St George's Day! He was buried "full 17 foot deep" in Holy Trinity Church, Stratford, and left an epitaph cursing anyone who dared disturb his bones.

There have been preposterous theories disputing Shakespeare's authorship. Some claim that Sir Francis Bacon (1561–1626), philosopher and Lord Chancellor, was the real author of Shakespeare's plays. Others propose Edward de Vere, Earl of Oxford (1550–1604), or, even more weirdly, Queen Elizabeth I. The implication is that the "real" Shakespeare had to be a university graduate or an aristocrat. Nothing less would do for the world's greatest writer.

Shakespeare is mysteriously hidden behind his work. His life will not tell us what inspired his genius.

EDITORIAL

Richard Appignanesi: Text Adaptor

Richard Appignanesi was a founder and co-director of the Writers & Readers Publishing Cooperative and Icon Books where he originated the internationally acclaimed *Introducing* series. His own best-selling titles in the series include *Freud*, *Postmodernism* and *Existentialism*. He is also the author of the fiction trilogy *Italia Perversa* and the novel *Yukio Mishima's Report to the Emperor*. Currently associate editor of the journal *Third Text* and reviews editor of the journal *Futures*, his latest book *What do Existentialists Believe?* was released in 2006.

Nick de Somogyi: Textual Consultant

Nick de Somogyi works as a freelance writer and researcher, as a genealogist at the College of Arms, and as a contributing editor to *New Theatre Quarterly*. He is the founding editor of the *Globe Quartos* series, and was the visiting curator at Shakespeare's Globe, 2003–6. His publications include *Shakespeare's Theatre of War* (1998), *Jokermen and Thieves: Bob Dylan and the Ballad Tradition* (1986), and (from 2001) the *Shakespeare Folios* series for Nick Hern Books. He has also contributed to the Open University (1995), Carlton Television (2000), and BBC Radio 3 and Radio 4.

ARTIST

Ilya

Ilya is a comic book writer and artist whose work has been published by Marvel, DC and Dark Horse in the USA, Kodansha in Japan, and numerous independent companies worldwide. His previous books include the *Manga Drawing Kit* for Thunder Bay Press; award-winning graphic novel series *The End of the Century Club*; *It's Dark in London* for Serpent's Tail; and *Skidmarks*, a charming kitchen-sink drama. Illustration clients include the BBC, Royal Academy of Arts, *The Times* and *The Guardian*, and most recently *East End Life*, for whom he crafts a regular strip. He also edits *The Mammoth Book of BEST NEW MANGA*.

PUBLISHER

SelfMadeHero is a UK-based manga and graphic novel imprint, reinventing some of the most important works of European and world literature. In 2008 SelfMadeHero was named **UK Young Publisher of the Year** at the prestigious British Book Industry Awards.

OTHER SELFMADEHERO TITLES:

EYE CLASSICS: *Nevermore*, *The Picture of Dorian Gray*, *The Trial*, *The Master and Margarita*, *Crime and Punishment*, *Dr. Jekyll and Mr. Hyde*.

SELF MADE HERO

www.selfmadehero.com